DK READERS

Level 2

Dinosaur Dinners
Fire Fighter!
Bugs! Bugs! Bugs!
Slinky, Scaly Snakes!
Animal Hospital
The Little Ballerina
Munching, Crunching, Sniffing,
    and Snooping
The Secret Life of Trees
Winking, Blinking, Wiggling,
    and Waggling
Astronaut: Living in Space
Twisters!
Holiday! Celebration Days
    around the World
The Story of Pocahontas
Horse Show
Survivors: The Night the
    Titanic Sank
Eruption! The Story of
    Volcanoes
The Story of Columbus
Journey of a Humpback Whale
Amazing Buildings
Feathers, Flippers, and Feet
LEGO: Castle Under Attack
LEGO: Rocket Rescue
¡Insectos! *en español*
Ice Skating Stars

Level 3

Spacebusters: The Race to
    the Moon
Beastly Tales
Shark Attack!
Titanic
Invaders from Outer Space
Movie Magic
Plants Bite Back!
Time Traveler
Bermuda Triangle
Tiger Tales
Aladdin
Heidi
Zeppelin: The Age of the
    Airship
Spies
Terror on the Amazon
Disasters at Sea
The Story of Anne Frank
Abraham Lincoln: Lawyer,
    Leader, Legend
George Washington: Soldier,
    Hero, President
Extreme Sports
Spiders' Secrets
The Big Dinosaur Dig
Space Heroes: Amazing
    Astronauts
LEGO: Mission to the Arctic
NFL: Super Bowl Heroes
NFL: Peyton Manning
MLB: Home Run Heroes: Big
    Mac, Sammy, and Junior
MLB: Roberto Clemente
MLB: Roberto Clemente
    en español
MLB: World Series Heroes
MLB: Record Breakers

A Note to Parents

DK READERS is a compelling program for beginning readers, designed in conjunction with leading literacy experts, including Dr. Linda Gambrell, Director of the Eugenge T. Moore School of Education at Clemson University. Dr. Gambrell has served on the Board of Directors of the International Reading Association and as President of the National Reading Conference.

Beautiful illustrations and superb full-color photographs combine with engaging, easy-to-read stories to offer a fresh approach to each subject in the series. Each DK READER is guaranteed to capture a child's interest while developing his or her reading skills, general knowledge, and love of reading.

The five levels of DK READERS are aimed at different reading abilities, enabling you to choose the books that are exactly right for your child:

Pre-level 1: Learning to read
Level 1: Beginning to read
Level 2: Beginning to read alone
Level 3: Reading alone
Level 4: Proficient readers

The "normal" age at which a child begins to read can be anywhere from three to eight years old, so these levels are only a general guideline.

No matter which level you select, you can be sure that you are helping your child learn to read, then read to learn!

LONDON, NEW YORK, MUNICH,
MELBOURNE, and DELHI

Senior Art Editor Cheryl Telfer
Designer Sadie Thomas
Series Editor Deborah Lock
U.S. Editor Elizabeth Hester
Production Shivani Pandey
Picture Researcher
Sarah Stewart-Richardson
DTP Designer Almudena Díaz
Jacket Designer Chris Drew

Reading Consultant
Linda Gambrell, Ph.D.

First American Edition, 2004
04 05 06 07 08 10 9 8 7 6 5 4 3
Published in the United States by DK Publishing, Inc.
375 Hudson Street, New York, New York 10014

Published in Great Britain by Dorling Kindersley Limited

Library of Congress Cataloging-in-Publication Data
Lock, Deborah.
Feathers flippers and feet / by Deborah Lock.-- 1st American ed.
p. cm. -- (DK readers)
ISBN 0-7566-0265-3 (hc) -- ISBN 0-7566-0264-5 (pbk.)
1. Animal locomotion--Juvenile literature. [1. Animal
locomotion. 2.Animals--Habits and behavior.]
I. Title. II. Series: Dorling Kindersley readers.
QP301.L675 2004
591.47'9--dc22
                              2003016722

Color reproduction by Colourscan, Singapore
Printed and bound in China by L Rex Printing Co., Ltd.

The publisher would like to thank the following for
their kind permission to reproduce their images:
Position key: c=center; b=bottom; l=left; r=right; t=top
Getty Images: Anup Shah 1, John Giustina 6-7, Tim Flach 6tr,
Jeff Hunter 14, 16, Paul Souders 18, Eastcott Momatiuk 28-29;
Corbis: Wolfgang Kaehler 3, Lynda Richardson 8, Jeffrey L.
Rotman, 21t, W. Perry Conway 21c, 32tl, Robert Pickett 28b,
Renee Lynn 30-31, Buddy Mays 31t, Kevin Schafer 32cr;
N.H.P.A.: Stephen Dalton 4-5, 6tl, Linda Pitkin 14-15, Keven
Schafer, 21b; **Alamy Images:** Chris Caldicott 5r, Steve Bloom 32bl;
DK Picture Library: Jerry Young 9cr, 10, 11c, 27t, Drusillas Zoo
23t, Philip Dowell 28c; **Ecoscene:** Lando Pescatori 13b, Visual &
Written 20; **Nature Picture Library Ltd:** Jeff Rotman 15c, Peter
Blackwell 30t, Brandon Cole 30c;
All other images © Dorling Kindersley Limited
For further information see: www.dkimages.com

Discover more at

www.dk.com

DK READERS

BEGINNING
2
TO READ ALONE

Feathers, flippers, and feet

Written by Deborah Lock

DK Publishing, Inc.

All around the world,
animals are moving—flying
in the air, crawling on land,
or swimming in the oceans.

Animals move
to catch food.

Animals move
to explore their
environment.

Animals move to
escape danger.

Come take a closer
look at the different
and unusual ways
animals get around.

Wings are for flying
high in the air.
Wings are for preening,
parading, and flapping.

Wings are for swooping,
SOARING, and
gliding.

Wings are for darting, flitting, and fluttering.

Wings are for catching the *breeze.*

Whose feathers are these?
Try to guess.

He struts proudly around
and has a long, colorful train
that he can raise like a fan.

She silently swoops down on her prey at night.

His graceful feathers are soft and white.

His colorful feathers are very bright.

Flying high

To fly, birds not only flap their wings, but also open and close the gaps between their feathers.

Were you right? Let's find out.

A peacock shows off his colorful feathers to attract a mate.

The soft feathers of the barn owl are shaped to muffle the sound of the wing beats.

A swan is born with gray feathers, which gradually turn to snowy white.

Parrot feathers contain chemicals that reflect the light to give off amazing colors.

Not all wings are made of feathers.

Amazingly, a bumblebee's small, fine wings can lift its heavy body.

Buzzzzzzzz

How do bees fly?
Bees do not flap their wings, but flip them forward and backward to create a lifting effect.

When a leaf butterfly closes its wings, it looks just like a leaf—a perfect disguise!

Can you see it?

A ladybug has another pair of wings underneath its red, spotted pair.

Flippers are for
swimming through
the water.

Flippers are for
leaping, swirling,
and splashing.

Flippers are for dodging,
dashing, and chasing.

Flippers are for paddling,
flipping, and rolling.
Flippers are for darting away.

Whose flippers are these?

An ocean giant is on a long trip.
He spends winter in the Caribbean
and summer in the Arctic.

Her long front
flippers provide
her with speed.

He waddles
on land, but
swims with ease.

Look carefully
at this one—
it's tricky.

Flippers and fins
Flippers are the
arm bones of
ocean mammals.
Fins are not
supported by bones.

Were you right? Let's find out.

A humpback whale has the longest flippers of any animal.

A sea lion has two pairs
of flippers that help
her move quickly on
land and in water.

A penguin is a flightless
bird whose wings
are used as
flippers.

A diver wears flippers
to swim down into
deep water to
explore a wreck or
an underwater cave.

Ocean mammals can also use their flippers to do other things.

A manatee uses its flippers to hold on to its food.

A dolphin uses its flippers to make friendly contact with its young.

A seal uses its flippers to push itself forward on land.

Burying eggs
Each year, sea turtles visit the same beach to lay their eggs. They use their flippers to bury them in the sand.

Feet are for moving
around on land.

Feet are for running,
jumping, and
leaping.

Feet are for
walking,
waddling,
and sliding.

Feet are for
climbing,
clinging, and
grasping.

Feet are for
scampering
away.

Whose feet are these?

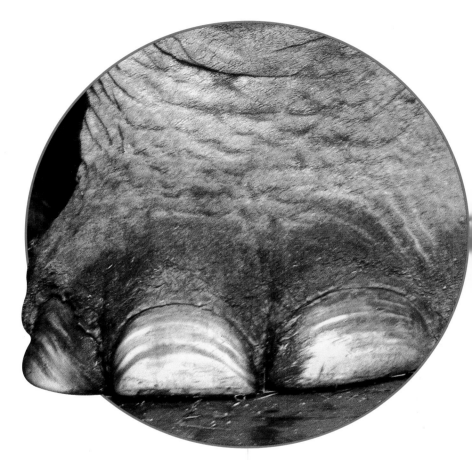

He is the heaviest animal on land.
He uses his great big feet
to loosen the plants he eats
because he has no hands.

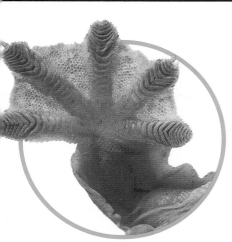

He's a small tropical lizard who can walk across a ceiling.

You'll find her in the water quacking, splashing, and swimming.

He gets bigger and bigger as he just keeps on eating.

Were you right? Let's find out.
An elephant spreads his huge
weight across his four feet.

A gecko's feet are covered with tiny hairs, which help him to slide along any surface without slipping.

"Quack!"

When swimming, a duckling uses her webbed feet like paddles.

A caterpillar has sucker-like feet with small claws on the end for gripping the leaves he's eating.

What else can
animals do with
their feet?

A tree frog has
suckers on its feet
that stick to
any surface.

A water
boatman can
float on water by
spreading out its feet.

Birds of prey catch
food with their
clawed feet, which
are called talons.

Dogs use
their paws to
scratch an itch.

Who holds the records?

A Ruppell's Griffon vulture was flying at 37,000 feet (11,277 meters) when it hit an airplane.

The sperm whale makes the deepest dives of any animal.

The slowest
mammal is the
three-toed
sloth, who spends
most of the day
hanging from branches asleep.

When chasing its prey, a cheetah
can reach speeds of 65 miles per
hour (105 kilometers per hour).

Fascinating facts

The wandering albatross has the longest wingspan of any bird.

A butterfly uses its feet to taste whether food is good enough to eat.

Although an ostrich has fluffy feathers, it cannot fly. Instead, it struts on long legs.

Unlike monkeys, the sifaka has to bounce as if it were on a trampoline because its arms are shorter than its legs.

A walrus has rough, thick skin on the bottom of its flippers to grip when it moves on rocks or ice.

When they are angry, rhinos can charge faster than an Olympic sprinter.

Index